Soren's Story

A Parable About Bullies
and the Peaceable Kingdom

Written by Al Niese ❧ *Illustrated by Amy Gagnon*

Al Niese

Soren's Story: A Parable About Bullies and the Peaceable Kingdom
Copyright © 2021 Al Niese

ISBN: 978-1-63381-244-4

This is a work of fiction. Names, characters, places, and incidents either are the product of the author's imagination or are used fictitiously, and any resemblance to actual persons, living or dead, is coincidental.

Illustrations by Amy Gagnon

Designed and produced by:
Maine Authors Publishing
12 High Street, Thomaston, Maine
www.maineauthorspublishing.com

Printed in the United States of America

Dedicated to Bronda M. Niese

and

In memory of Alfred M. Niese Sr., who bought his two young sons their first pairs of pigeons

*People just don't make the connection between the
dove of peace and the pigeon in the street.*

—Jean Hansell, author of *The Pigeon in the Wider World*

The Bridge

The first sound I ever knew was a feeling.

It was the feeling of a thud, of a bang, a bump-bump-bump.

Some days later, I began to understand the feeling, for I struggled free from my shell, my first home, out into the nest my parents had created for us under a highway bridge.

My nest-mate and sister soon joined me, pecking open her shell. Our parents took the empty shells from our nest and dropped them onto the roadway below.

When my eyes began to open, I saw, of course, Mother and Father—gray and blue, with neck-flecks of purple and green.

Later I saw what I had felt all around me, above and below— scary, noisy things—and big! Cars and trailers with trucks pulling them hard, motorcycles blasting, buses roaring.

From city streets, Mother and Father brought food to us, opening their beaks to expel into our open mouths what they found for us. Best of all, they fed us corn and other seeds, sometimes dropped by friendly human hands in the park.

We are city pigeons.

My name is Soren. My sister is Molly. And as we grew, my sister and I, day by day, noticed our feathers pushing through their quills and then, at last, blooming, a little like the way we would see flowers do.

Yet soon, we would have to fly out from under the highway bridge to another home somewhere. Mother and Father told us the flight would be dangerous. "You must seize the right moment," they said. "You need to fly over the cars, or between them, and between the trailers and the buses. The buses and trucks will be your greatest challenge."

"Courage!" Mother and Father said. "Pump your wings often so they become strong! Flap them many times for practice. Use your eyes and look both ways. And only when the way is clear, then lean forward into the noisy, windy air. Trust your wings, and fly out of the tunnel—and into the light."

In the Park—Friends and Bullies

Molly flew off first, with great courage. But immediately, and much too fast, a bus roared beneath me. As I watched from our nest, I lost sight of Molly. I feared the bus might hit her—or even carry her away from me forever.

The very next day, I tried too. Leaning forward, trusting in my wing muscles, my new feathers, and all my practice, I looked both ways, chose the moment, pushed off, and flew... out from under the bridge into the sunlight, into a world of blue and green, of buildings and trees, and of people.

Some time later, I saw Mother and Father. And I found food where they did, between the feet of people going to work, people coming home tired, people scurrying, turning, even running sometimes as they went. And some were eating, too, hurrying between the buildings, dropping crumbs and other pieces of food as they went.

I kept looking for Molly all the while, and, finally, to my great relief and delight, I found her in the great city park. Together, we made friends there, human friends, pigeon friends. Among them was a brave pigeon who looked much like us except that he had wings of entirely white feathers. We learned his name: Bright Wings.

One day, when a few kind children were enjoying watching us, two others, cruel boys, came with pebbles and stones. They threw them at me and my friends and hollered, "Dirty!" and, "Bad Pigeons."

But Bright Wings tried to stop the bullies, courageously standing up to them on the sidewalk, his chest out, refusing to shrink back in fear. Though I'd thought him very wise before, I suddenly thought him foolish for taking such a risk. One boy hit Bright Wings in the head with a stone, and Bright Wings fluttered, dropping to the pavement among the stones that fell beside him.

The bullies that day became Molly's and my enemies. We feared them, hated them.

But two of the friendly children in the park, Cecily and Sarah, shouted to the bullies, "Stop!" The bullies, much to our surprise, ran away. The girls, ever so tenderly, wrapped Bright Wings in their mother's scarf. Limp in their hands, he did not move a feather. Where they took him, we could not tell.

As hard as we tried, we could not accept that this was the way the life of our white-winged friend would come to an end.

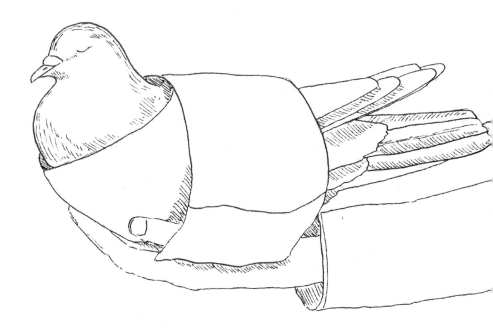

What Bright Wings Taught Us

In sadness, Molly and I began to appreciate how brave, really, Bright Wings had been. In time, we recalled many wise things Bright Wings had taught us: "Wherever you go, Soren and Molly, I hope you will remember what my parents one day told me: 'We pigeons are not bad; we are not dirty. Do not believe it!'"

"Remember always," Bright Wings said, "that we belong to the Great Spirit who made us. We did not make ourselves. We pigeons are the rock doves of times long gone by, when many of us nested on rocky ledges by the sea and other natural places.

"The great passenger pigeons, millions of them, were of our kind. They were sometimes hunted by people to eat, or sometimes just for fun. There are none left anywhere alive on Earth today. Not one.

"Many of us actually are loved by people," Bright Wings said. "They like the way some of us tumble like acrobats in the air—tumblers, they call us. Some of us, called homers, can fly hundreds of miles in a day, as fast as cars. And some of us can fly upward in flocks to such heights that people can see us only as tiny dots high in the sky!

"And people love to see us return home to the lofts they build for us on rooftops in cities, and in yards outside cities in villages and towns. We come in all colors, and shapes, some of us with beautiful tails, graceful necks, and even feather-crowns on our heads. Some of us look a little silly, really.

"We sometimes have flown with searchers in airplanes. Our keen eyes helped pilots find people swimming or floating on life rafts after their boats have sunk below the waves. The swift, strong beat of our wings carried messages in little leg tubes to save soldiers in times when people fight, as so often they do. They even call such pigeons heroes.

"But unlike people, we doves and pigeons are peaceful, not warlike. And we get dirty only from people's sticky litter in the streets, from oil in puddles, from chimney smoke, and from the black air that noisy trucks sometimes blow out. When we get sick, Soren and Molly, it is mostly from things that people do to us. So never think of us, or of yourselves, as awful. Never!"

Bright Wings also told us he'd learned this: "Many good people want to make the earth clean and bright and safe. It is their gift to the Great Spirit who made not just people—but every living thing. The Great Spirit wants all people to have room, to have life, to care and have peace.

"Bravely, the Great Spirit also took a chance, leaving it to people to make choices to follow, or refuse to follow, what wise ones in ancient times taught them about kindness and fairness, about being humble and living thankfully."

New Life in the Old Meeting House

Molly and I said goodbye to Mother and Father. We touched our beaks to theirs one last time, and then flew from the park, leaving them and our friends behind—as well as the bullies.

We flew over fields and woods and came upon an old wooden meeting house on a hill. It had a tower that reached toward the clouds. Within it, there was a great bell with a clapper that made the bell ring out over the hills whenever its rope was pulled from below. But the bell, its rope long ago broken, had not been rung for many years.

Up in the bell tower, a caretaker who noticed us made a space for us in a corner. She loved pigeons from her childhood days. She spread straw and left us food and water for the first night.

We soon found other food, of course: wheat and many other kinds of seeds in the surrounding meadows, as we pigeons have always done.

From our belfry home, we could see down, between great wooden beams, to the floor below. On special occasions, people of all kinds would gather, coming from miles around. Sometimes there was mostly silence; at other times there would be wonderful sounds—singing, like our own cooing sounds, but fuller and louder.

And the people who gathered in the meeting house below sometimes made a sound like the wind: "Holy," they said. They spoke of forgiveness and mercy, and they gave thanks for life to the Great Spirit, maker of us all—for blessings, but also for challenges to be better, to do better.

At times, they looked into each other's faces and said, "Peace," meaning, "Whatever has happened that made us enemies, may we take courage to speak to each other of such things, and listen, and find a better way to be." They talked about letting go of grudges and revenge.

Molly and I could feel it was not easy for the people to do this. Their struggle seemed a little like our own in leaving our nest under the bridge—and taking to our wings for the very first time. Yet love and hope filled the old meeting house, and us, that day with warmth and light.

Among those who came to the meeting house one day were the two girls, Sarah and Cecily who had been our friends, the ones who wrapped Bright Wings in their mother's scarf. And there, also, were the two boys who were their enemies, and ours too, on that day they bullied us and called us names in the park.

All four came with Sarah and Cecily's mother. She wanted the enemies to come together—to find some way to make peace. It took a while, but the people there reached out to each other with forgiveness that day. The four children did it, too, looking softly into each other's eyes. Sarah and Cecily's mother was glad; her hope in bringing the children to the old meeting house seemed fulfilled.

World Day of Thanksgiving: The Peaceable Kingdom

How much later I cannot tell, for time is a great mystery to me, but one day, the best of all days finally came. It was the World Day of Thanksgiving. People came to the old meeting house and formed a great circle. But they didn't come just to the meeting house.

All over the world people came together in all kinds of places—to give thanks. We did not make ourselves, they said. They said thank you to the Giver—some of them said it to one they called the Great Spirit. And something happened. They had the feeling they belonged together, to each other. What began in thanksgiving ended in love.

People's skin, their hair, their clothes were all different colors that day in the old meeting house. They wore different symbols around their necks. Where they came from, or what they thought, or did, who their mothers and fathers were, or what their houses looked like—these things didn't seem to matter to them anymore. They were brothers and sisters, they said. Like Molly and me.

They spoke of a lion "lying down with the lamb," of turning swords into tools for tilling the soil—strange things like that.

"The war is over at last," they said. "The war between people, and war on the land with all its living things, too. War is done!" they said. "Love has won," they said. And the Peaceable Kingdom, long yearned for and worked for, had come. "It had been within us all the time."

Some brought animals to the meeting house that day from their homes and farms, creatures great and small, including doves.

Nor did they quarrel over things like whether "Great Spirit" was the right name for the Giver. Named or unnamed, that spirit was among them. They just knew it.

Mercy was there. Grace was there. The people ceased to argue over who was good or bad. "For all of us, to be sure, are something of both," they said.

And with my sister Molly at my side, I looked down through the meeting house roof beams and saw below the different people in all their different colors and sizes and clothes and shapes, and all the animals, too. And a feeling came upon me the way a feeling sometimes just comes to us:

> "O happy living things! no tongue
> Their beauty might declare:
> A spring of love gushed from my heart,
> And I blessed them unaware."

I hardly knew what I was doing.

Then I looked past the bell through the opening in the old belfry, and up against the sky, sailing high, what did I see? I saw...Bright Wings! Molly and I had feared him dead from the bully's stones, but instead he was high aloft on his white wings.

He suddenly came down and flew through the archway of the meeting house door. As if to meet us, he rose high up toward the belfry, flying just beneath us, then circled down, finally hovering above the people while they watched him, just hanging there in the air.

People were so filled with wonderment at the sight that no one spoke a word, or even felt the need to.

Nor did anyone quite know how to explain it, but the great bell in the meeting house tower, long silent, began to move and then to swing and ring out over the hills and into the towns around and way beyond.

"Hope on," it said. Gong!

"Do justice and love kindness." Gong!

"Take courage and confront evil," it rang out. Gong!

"And remember mercy." Gong!

"In truth and mercy is our hope." Gong!

**Let there at last be thanksgiving,
fairness, and peace on Earth.**

**And may the Spirit ever hover over
us all on—bright wings!**

Concerning *Soren's Story* as Parable

British dove/dovecote scholar and pigeon advocate Jean Hansell (her books are listed elsewhere here for reference) helps us "make the connection between the dove of peace and the pigeon in the street." Soren's Story seeks to do the same. As a parable about power and peace, it presents us with a lens for viewing our lives, society, and history.

This children's story is written in appreciation of the pigeon, or the rock dove, an extraordinary creature and universal symbol of world peace in ancient literature and even today.* On various levels of meaning, the story is about bullying and forgiveness, courage, self-esteem, hope, and justice. It is about thankfulness, the Great Spirit, and how we the people can do better.

The pigeon is the among the most revered of birds and, it has been said, the most reviled—especially the city pigeon (see Andrew D. Blechman's 2006 book *Pigeons*). The author of *Soren's Story* was born in New York City, raised pigeons as a boy, and flew a small flock of high-flyers, or tipplers, in New Jersey as a young adult.

The tale's interreligious, inclusive intent was inspired in part by the interfaith throng that gathered shortly after the tragic fall of the twin towers on 9/11 in Yankee Stadium. While the major religions of the world were represented, nonreligious people and humanists of differing philosophical and spiritual views were there as well.

Soren's Story would remind us of the words of Archbishop Desmond Tutu of South Africa: "There is no future without forgiveness." The story places his assertion in a context that children know and can enter: bullying by the powerful of those lacking power to protect their own life and dignity. Bullying is one illustration of hubris—our human propensity to "confuse natural self-affirmation with destructive self-elevation." (Paul Tillich)

Soren recalls, in the last chapter, Noah's dove and all the creatures of the Ark in Genesis. The story's conclusion invokes the Hebrew prophets, honored by Jews, Christians, and Muslims. It recalls the prophetic images of swords beaten into plowshares and spears into pruning hooks, images of the lion and lamb, the wolf and the kid, lying down together.

Central to the story is Bright Wings, a pigeon whose name comes from the final line of Gerard Manley Hopkins's poem "God's Grandeur." Bright Wings becomes the story's symbol of the Peaceable Kingdom, the coming of which was envisioned by the prophets. As the late Elijah Cummings reminded us: We can do better, we are better, than this.

The story quotes directly from another important poem of the English language, Samuel Taylor Coleridge's *The Rime of the Ancient Mariner*. The Hopkins and Coleridge poems both summon us to humility and thanksgiving—to the sure acknowledgement that clever as we earthlings can be, we did not, after all, make ourselves.

The parable envisions a universal celebration—a World Day of Thanksgiving—and affirms that, spiritually speaking, love can flow from the act of giving humble thanks together. Thanksgiving is thus elevated to being on a plane with the highest virtue—love.

The recent book, Andrew Garn's *The New York Pigeon: Behind the Feathers*, was reviewed in the *New York Times*. An excerpt from that appraisal: "While most New Yorkers spend their time avoiding pigeons, Andrew Garn spends his getting as close as possible. His work dignifies the maligned bird." So do the efforts of myriad volunteers in the US and Europe, who by various creative means (e.g., urban dovecotes) help sustain and manage healthy wild pigeon flocks.

The books of Jean Hansell illuminate the five-thousand-year history of the bird in Eastern and Western civilization. Multiple images of the dove (e.g., love, wisdom, hope, truth, peace) flow from Dr. Hansell's writings. But what emerges at the same time is a common symbol—one in which different countries, religions, and widely varying cultures meet.

*The terms pigeon and dove can be used interchangeably, both referring to Columba livia, though dove is "traditionally reserved for the aesthetic contexts of religion, literature, and art, while pigeon applies to matters such as sport, fancy birds, and culinary use..." —Jean Hansell

For Further Reading and Reference

Poems

- Samuel Taylor Coleridge, *The Rime of the Ancient Mariner*
- Gerard Manley Hopkins, "God's Grandeur"

Books on the Pigeon (Rock dove)

- Andrew D. Blechman, *Pigeons: The Fascinating Saga of the World's Most Revered and Reviled Bird*, 2006
- Andrew Garn, *The New York Pigeon: Behind the Feathers*, 2019
- Jean Hansell, *The Pigeon in the Wider World*, 2010; *The Pigeon in History*, 1998; *Images of the Dove*, 2003; *Doves and Dovecotes*, 1988 (with Peter Hansell)
- Wendell Levi, *The Pigeon*, 1941/1957

Other Readings and Resources for Reference

- Diogenes Allen, *The Path of Perfect Love*, 1992
- Karen Armstrong, *Twelve Steps to the Compassionate Life*, 2010
- *The New Oxford Annotated Bible with the Apocrypha*, 1991
- Frederick Buechner, *Beyond Words*, 2004
- John Ciardi, *How Does a Poem Mean*, 1959
- Christie Palmer Lowrance, *Nature's Ambassador: The Legacy of Thornton W. Burgess*, 2013

- Brian MacLaren, *A Generous Orthodoxy*, 2004
- Bill McKibben, *The End of Nature*, 1989
- Guy Merchant, Director, Bird Consultancy Control Services International (BCCSi), Ely, Cambridgeshire, UK
- Robert Corin Morris, *Wrestling with Grace*, 2003
- Reinhold Niebuhr, *The Irony of American History*, 1952
- William G. Sayres, *The Discourse of Gratitude in the Novels of Jane Austen* (University of New Hampshire), 1995
- Sherman Brothers—song from the movie *Mary Poppins*, "Feed the Birds"
- Edmund Hamilton Sears, "It Came Upon a Midnight Clear," 1846
- Paul Tillich, *The Essential Tillich*, ed. F. Forrester Church, 1999
- Archbishop Desmond Tutu, *No Future Without Forgiveness*, 1999; *God Is Not a Christian: And Other Provocations*, 2011
- David Foster Wallace, Commencement Address at Kenyon College, 2005
- Cornel West, *Black Prophetic Fire*, 2005
- Richard Wile, *Requiem in Stones*, 2016

About the Author

AL NIESE AND HIS WIFE, BRONDA, LIVE in Brunswick. Their two children and their families also live in Maine. A former board chair of Mid Coast Hunger Prevention Program (MCHPP), Al served Episcopal churches in Maine after leading urban and suburban churches in New Jersey. His interests include community mental health, the United Nations, comparative religion, sailing, antique reed organs—and tippler pigeons.

About the Illustrator

AMY GAGNON LIVES IN RURAL MAINE, where she lives in a Victorian era farmhouse. Her work combines her interests in art and nature as well as history and storytelling. She creates pieces ranging from small illustrations to wall-size murals. She also enjoys gardening and playing traditional fiddle music.